12 Strategies

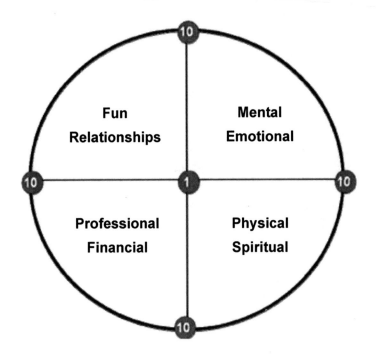

Fun
Relationships

Mental
Emotional

Professional
Financial

Physical
Spiritual

This is an effective system for achieving the abundance, prosperity, and wealth that you require to live the lifestyle that you desire.

by **Willie C. Hooks**

XULON PRESS

12 Strategies for Success
by Willie C. Hooks

Printed in the United States of America

ISBN 9781625095961

www.xulonpress.com

The decision to succeed is a very personal one.

The 12 Strategies for Success is more than a book. It is, in fact, an effective system that will support you in achieving the life that you want, need, and desire.

Imagine what you could accomplish,
the life you could lead . . .

Simply turn the page to begin the journey . . .

Contents

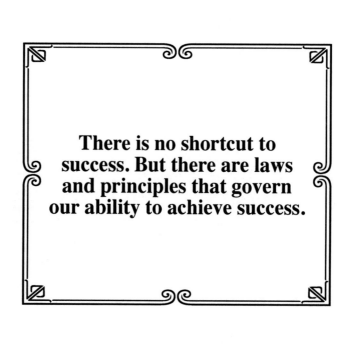

There is no shortcut to success. But there are laws and principles that govern our ability to achieve success.

Introduction

꧂

It seems like everywhere I turn I hear someone asking about the shortcut to success. There is no shortcut to success. But there are laws and principles that govern our ability to achieve success. By success, I just mean accomplishing the goal that we select, hopefully one that we desire. When followed, the *12 Strategies For Success* significantly increase our chances of achieving the goals that we seek. So in a kind of funny way, understanding and following the *12 Strategies For Success* is *indeed* the shortcut to accomplishing the goals that we seek.

That is exactly why this life-changing book to achieve your goals was written. These laws are timeless, pragmatic, practical, but more importantly, they simply work. And they work consistently in direct proportion to our application of them. If we apply them—they work. If we don't, we will struggle to achieve our goals and receive inconsistent results.

So it's to everyone's advantage to learn the *12 Strategies for Success* and to apply them consistently each and every day. Because there is nothing more rewarding than living the life that we desire. And that desire is manifested through goal achievement.

When I talk with people that have a great deal of frustration and stress, it's usually because they're not living the life that they truly desire. There are many reasons why that's so. Some will say it's because they don't have the money to support the lifestyle they want. Others will say they don't have the time to do what they want to do. Regardless of the reason, if they truly understood and implemented the *12 Strategies for Success*, its implementation would go a long way toward

The 12 Strategies for Success will significantly increase our chances of achieving the goals that we seek.

helping them overcome whatever barriers that may be blocking them from living the life they want.

The aim of this book is to support you in achieving the goals and that life that you want with ease. In fact, when you have completed the exercises in this book, you'll be able:

- To understand what a balanced life is for you and how to achieve it,
- To get clear on your goals and understand how to consistently set and achieve them,
- To learn to take consistent actions toward your goals,
- To overcome barriers, obstacles, and challenges in your life that interfere with your goal achievement, and
- To develop the right mental attitude to keep you motivated and making progress towards goal attainment.

The fastest path to achieving the lifestyle that you desire is through the application of the twelve strategies.

Let's begin your extraordinary journey to achieving the goals that you desire.

To be an effective tool, the KRAs must be consistent with how you think about your life, and therefore, the KRAs must be personalized for each one of us.

The Personal Life Balance Wheel

The purpose of the Personal Life Balance Wheel is to graphically imprint upon your mind the balance present in your life. Review the spokes on the wheel in the diagram that represent the eight major areas of your life. These should be the key areas that you want to achieve results in.

The wheel's spokes, the major areas of your life, are referred to as 'Key Result Areas' (KRAs). If these KRAs don't work for you, simply change the labels on the spokes to be reflective of the major areas that you'd prefer to focus on for results. To be an effective tool, the KRAs must be consistent with how you think about your life, and therefore, the KRAs must be personalized for each one of us.

Each KRA is listed on a scale of 1–10 (with 10 being the highest rating, 1 the lowest). Review each KRA and rate your assessment of that area, placing a dot on the spoke at the appropriate place to mark your rating. For example, if you assessed your mental KRA as being an 8, you would place a dot at the 8 position on the mental spoke. Then you would do the same for the rest of the KRAs until they are all marked with a dot at the appropriate rating.

Next, start at the twelve o'clock position and draw a line clockwise connecting the dots—the ones you just placed on the spokes as your personal assessments.

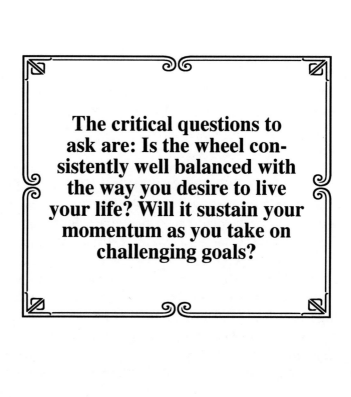

The critical questions to ask are: Is the wheel consistently well balanced with the way you desire to live your life? Will it sustain your momentum as you take on challenging goals?

Once connected, the dots represent a wheel reflective of the balance currently in your life based on your KRAs. The critical questions to ask are: Is the wheel consistently well balanced with the way you desire to live your life? Will it sustain your momentum as you take on challenging goals? Because if you're living a balanced life according to the areas that you're saying are the most important in your life, it should be balanced enough to roll.

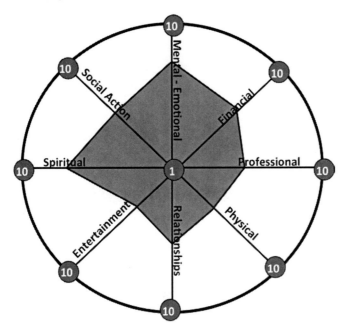

Keep this wheel with your goal-planning materials, and adjust your KRAs and your wheel accordingly. *Remember, this assessment is for your eyes only!* This tool is not for beating yourself up. Instead, it is to support you in making the right decisions to create the right level of balance in your life. The focus is on the right level of balance for you—what is appropriate for *you*—not someone else.

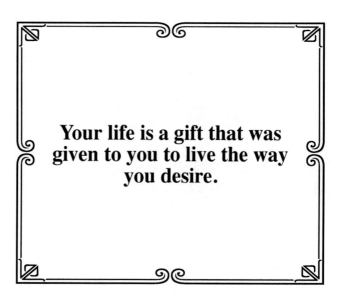

Your life is a gift that was given to you to live the way you desire.

Don't let anyone tell you what the right mix or the correct balance are for you, because no one else really knows your purpose and what you were put here to do.

Always remember that your life is a gift that was given to you to live the way you desire.

My Personal Life Balance Wheel

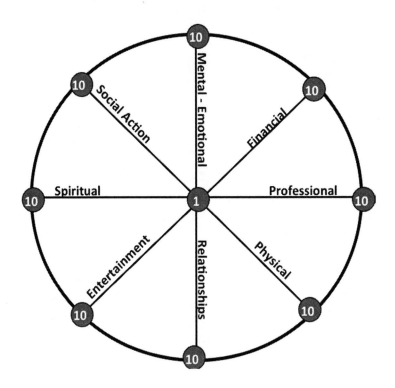

I will schedule daily action toward my number one goal, and start that action NOW! I cannot afford to wait until I feel right and everything is perfect before I start action

Chapter 2: Strategy 1

How To Develop
The Action Habit

A ction! I know ninety percent of all achievement comes from *daily action* toward the next thing I want. Daily action toward the next thing I want is absolutely necessary, an imperative *law* to become successful, wealthy and happy. This means taking one step every day toward the next thing I want. It means scheduling and *doing* something every day toward my goal. Today is the only day of opportunity. I must get rid of that feeling that there will be another day. I will not put off the decision, the action, and the opportunity. I will do it *today*. There is no tomorrow. I must keep moving, hustling, changing, and motivating myself to be happy and wealthy.

Thoughts alone never achieve success. I will schedule daily action toward my number one goal, and start that action NOW! I cannot afford to wait until I feel right and everything is perfect before I start action. I will start it now. Success is daily action toward the next thing I want. This means daily action with my brain, my heart, my body, my voice, my money, and most important of all — my time. I will constantly thrive on work. My mind never rest. I will undertake anything, have no fear, and let nothing stop me. I think nothing of picking up the phone and calling anybody in the world. The word *can't* does not exist for me. I have taken the word *failure out of my vocabulary*.

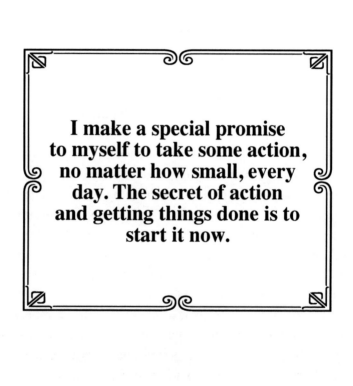

I make a special promise
to myself to take some action,
no matter how small, every
day. The secret of action
and getting things done is to
start it now.

If something cannot be done one way, I will do it another way, a better way. I will outwork any other person in the world. When others
are sleeping, I work. I live with energy, go to bed with energy, and get up with energy. I do much. I press hard and am in perpetual motion. I do what the failures do not like to do. Life is too short to be a failure.

I must want something with a burning desire that will not be denied. I want something strong enough to take some action, no matter how small, every day. The secret of action and getting things done is to start it now. All I have to do is start. I will do just one little thing, but I will start it now. I make a special promise to myself to take some action, no matter how small, every day. The secret of action and getting things done is to start it now. All I have to do is start. I will do just one little thing, but I will start it now. I make a special promise to myself to take some action toward my number one goal today. I write down my promise and the words, "START IT NOW." This promise will be one of my affirmations that I read three times a day.

Soon these three words, "START IT NOW," will get into my subconscious mind and start a thought habit. Each day, I will find myself doing more and more toward my number one burning desire.

I will remember, none of the universal laws for success will work unless I *start it now*.

When I do twice as much, I have to receive twice as much. This is a scientific law of the universe. Of course, all action toward my next goal must be planned. A plan of action must be written down on the pages of my notebook.

On the first page, I will write the words My Plan of Action. I will write my goal and the date I plan to have it completed.

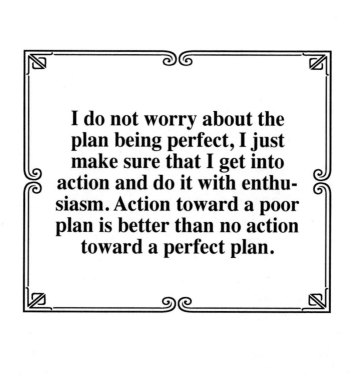

I do not worry about the plan being perfect, I just make sure that I get into action and do it with enthusiasm. Action toward a poor plan is better than no action toward a perfect plan.

On the next page, I write Step One. I write the action that I will take, and the date of its completion.

On the next page, I will write Step Two, the action I will take and the date of its completion.

I take as many pages of my notebook as I need, but I will plan my steps; I will write them down and the date of their completion. As I finish each step, I tear out the page and throw it away. I do not worry about the plan being perfect, I just make sure that I get into action and do it with enthusiasm. Action toward a poor plan is better than no action toward a perfect plan.

Some physical action must be taken each day on my first step. When that step is completed, I go to the second step, and soon, all steps are completed and the planned goal is realized.

As I read this Law of Action, I must *know* that I am a person of action. I started action the moment I became interested enough in success and happiness to start this program. I am taking action by physically writing down my desires, my goals, my affirmations, and my plans to reach them. Inside is a burning desire to be someone. I want to make a difference in the world. I want to accomplish great things and make the world a better place for everyone.

The next time I take some action toward my next goal in life, I will feel proud. Enthusiasm grows and grows inside until it becomes a white heat of feeling and emotion. Every fiber of my being comes alive. My body, my mind, my heart, my soul, and all the power within me feels and knows that this is the right thing for me. I am headed in the right direction, and each time I take some action toward my goal, I get the same feeling of enthusiasm and power. Each time I say to myself, "start it now" and then take some action toward my goal, it goes into my beautiful subconscious mind and becomes a success habit.

Daily action toward the
next thing I want is a
key to success.

Some happy and wealthy people were asked to tell their greatest and most important secret about money making, and they replied, "Daily action toward the next thing I want." The key character of the wealthy is impatience. They want to make big things happen. Fast. They are driven by the urge of action. They hustle twice as fast as other people, and will not be stopped by the things that stop others.

Here are some fantastic secrets I will use to catapult me into each successful day:

1. Wake up. Play my affirmation or motivational audio for twenty to thirty minutes.

2. The instant the audio is over, do some form of light exercise, anything, but I will do some exercise. All the time I am doing exercises, I say to myself, "I have a strong, attractive, perfect body and each day it is becoming stronger, slimmer, and more attractive." I will suck in my stomach, puff out my chest, and flex my muscles.

3. Immediately after my exercise, I brush my teeth vigorously; look in the mirror and say, "I take care of my mouth so that only intelligent, positive statements will come out of my mouth. Only kind, helpful statements will come out of my beautiful mouth. My new mouth will issue only creative, beneficial, wealth-building, and happy words today."

4. Immediately after brushing my teeth, I rush into a warm stimulating shower and cleanse my body thoroughly. I say to myself while showering, "I have a brand new, beautiful, clean body that will make me wealthy and happy today."

Successful people hustle
twice as fast as other people,
and will not be stopped by
the things that stop others.

5. After my shower, I very vigorously dry my body with a large luxurious towel. I rub my whole body, face, and neck vigorously. I say to myself, "I am stimulating my blood to flow throughout my entire body, bringing color and fresh new blood for a vital skin and brain. The old tissue and thoughts are being rushed away to be replaced with the new, powerful, vibrant, exciting, wealthy, happy skin and brain I deserve today."

6. I dress completely, quickly, and say to myself, "My new beautiful, strong, attractive, vital, perfect, powerful, clean, vibrant, exciting, stimulating, and productive body, mouth, and brain deserve only the best clothes for such a wealthy, happy person as I am today."

7. I drink one glass of water only, absolutely no other food or drink, cigarettes or anything, and then go immediately to my own secluded quiet spot for my hour of goal setting and affirmations.

START IT NOW!

Notes:

Reflective Questions:
1. What is the secret to getting things done?
2. What actions will you take toward your number one goal?
3. How can you do twice as much so that you can achieve twice as much?

Sample Affirmations
- I live with energy, so I get things done.
- I take positive action toward my number one goal each day.
- I am making great progress toward my number one goal.
- I "Start It Now" in regards to making progress toward my number one goal

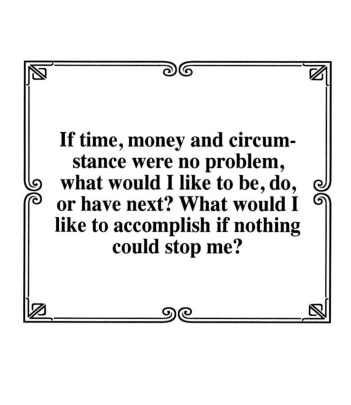

If time, money and circumstance were no problem,
what would I like to be, do,
or have next? What would I
like to accomplish if nothing
could stop me?

Chapter 3: Strategy 2

A Guide to Goal Setting

How to set and reach the right goals in your life are the most important steps towards success. There are two types of goals: tangible and intangible. Tangible goals are material things. Intangible goals are mental qualities. For example, a new home is a tangible goal, while honesty is an intangible goal.

To start setting goals for a happier and more successful life, make sure that you're alone and that everything is quiet. Turn off the music, the radio, and television. Take several sheets of paper to write on, and set aside at least one hour for this vital task.

Ask yourself the question, "If time, money, and circumstance were no problem, what would I like to be, do, or have next? What would I like to accomplish if nothing could stop me?" Write down everything that comes to mind, everything that you want to have and anything that you would like to do and that you want to be.

Here are a few qualities that you might desire: to be a person of action, to be persistent, to have a positive attitude, to have enthusiasm and love, to have the ability to say "no," and to have willpower.

Some professional goals might be: to be a doctor, a lawyer, an educator, self-employed, an effective sales person, a great leader or manager, a CEO, or a millionaire.

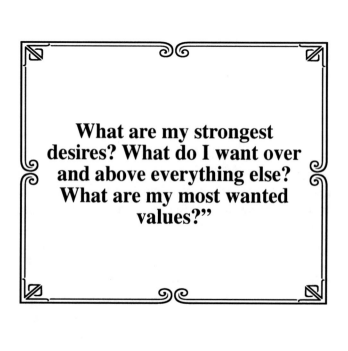

What are my strongest desires? What do I want over and above everything else? What are my most wanted values?"

Some physical goals might be: a home by the sea, a new car, and a million dollars in the bank.

The sky's the limit. You should think *big*. You can have anything you want to have, and you can be anything you want to be. You can have anything you want, provided that you:

1. Know exactly what you want,
2. Want it strongly enough,
3. Confidently expect to attain it,
4. Make it a top priority,
5. Focus your energies and attention on,
6. Change outdated habits, attitudes, behaviors, and expectations, and
7. Stop making excuses.

Consider the question of exactly what it is that you want. You must have a clear and full picture of your desires, aspirations, ambitions, and hopes. You must know which of a number of conflicting wants you desire more than the others. Take an assessment of yourself to determine which of these elements are the strongest.

Do this exercise with a pen and paper, asking yourself the following questions: What are my strongest desires? What do I want over and above everything else? What are my most wanted values?

Begin to write down your strongest desires as they come to mind. Make sure that you write everything that comes to mind while brainstorming, whether or not you really expect to be able to attain them. Put them all on the list, no matter how ridiculous or impossible they may seem at the moment. Bring to your consciousness all of the feelings, cravings, desires, and longings that have been dwelling in your subconscious mind.

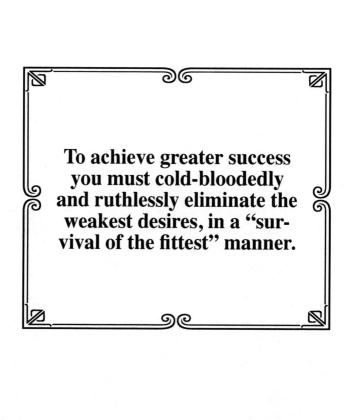

To achieve greater success
you must cold-bloodedly
and ruthlessly eliminate the
weakest desires, in a "survival of the fittest" manner.

The next step is to cold-bloodedly and ruthlessly eliminate the weakest desires, in a "survival of the fittest" manner. Those which remain will be the strongest. Review your list and strike off the weaker and less-insistent desires, as well as those which you recognize as bringing you only temporary satisfaction. Continue to trim the list until you feel that further pruning would result in cutting away "live wood."

When you reach this point, stop, and give yourself a much-needed mental rest. This rest will provide an opportunity for your subconscious to begin its work for you along its own particular lines.

When you pick up your list again, you'll find a new general order and arrangement of these items pictured in your mind. They will be grouped into several classes which you can compare with each other to help select certain desires which are stronger than the others. You will then eliminate the weaker classes, and make a new list consisting of the stronger remaining ones. After you've performed this exercise several times, with periods of rest and relaxation in between, you'll find you have a list of a few general classes of wishes. Your subconscious mind has been working its power upon the selection process, and at last, you're faced with just what you want!

Utilize the following three rules in your list trimming:

1. The Imperative Requisite: Consider if you want this one desirable thing at the sacrifice of another desirable thing, if you *really* want this thing–enough.
2. The Test of Full Desire: Weigh the value of this particular desire or class of desires in consideration of any immediate and future satisfaction. Your future satisfaction may be gained at the sacrifice or expense of your present satisfaction gained from this thing, or the reverse may be true.

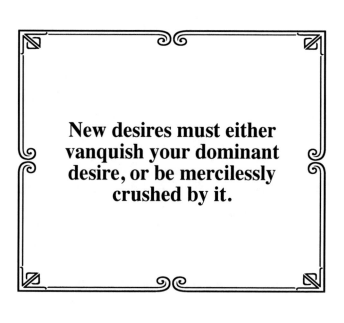

New desires must either
vanquish your dominant
desire, or be mercilessly
crushed by it.

3. The Depth of Desire: Eliminate superficial and transient emotions and desires, and instead, plunge into the deep places of your subconscious mind. Find the essential, basic, and permanent emotions and desires, which when aroused, are as persistent and imperative as the want of a suffocating person for air. These desires, your "Desire Giants," are the ones for which you will accept a high pay or cost value. These Giants will demand further consideration, and your power is now focused on these Giants. You must answer one question to further isolate your supreme desire and to help you concentrate your power on one ideal: "Will this desire tend to make me stronger, better, and more efficient?" To the degree that your mental state meets the requirements of this test, so too, is its degree of positivity and desirability. You have now determined the fittest of your desires, that *dominant desire* which will rule your emotional realm. Any new desires must either vanquish your dominant desire, or be mercilessly crushed by it. You now know exactly what you want, and how much you actually want it.

The next thing to do is to buy a very expensive loose-leaf notebook or journal of some kind with lots of pages. Buy the best one you can find, and one you like, because you must cherish it and treat it as the most important book in your life. A loose-leaf notebook works best so that pages can be added or removed as you grow and change. I recommend that you do *not* complete this process with a computer or any electronic device. There is something much more magical and powerful when pen and paper are used for goal setting: trust me on this critical point. It makes a big difference in the results that you will achieve and how fast the goal will be manifested.

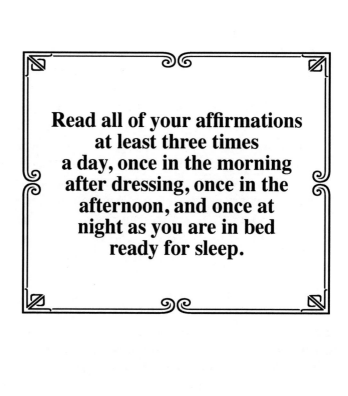

Read all of your affirmations
at least three times
a day, once in the morning
after dressing, once in the
afternoon, and once at
night as you are in bed
ready for sleep.

Next, make affirmations of all your tangible and intangible goals. An affirmation is a positive, present tense statement about my goal. Here's an example: "I live in my $1,000,000 dream house nestled among beautiful, towering trees on a high mountain overlooking the Pacific Ocean. There are six rooms and three bathrooms in my home, and on the northeast corner of my acre of heaven is a large 40' x 50' garage, containing my new Lexus convertible. I can see it very plainly. I can smell the piney atmosphere of this wonderful location. We love living in our dream-come-true home."

There is your affirmation. You can make as many affirmations as you have burning desires. It might take you many days, or even weeks, to get these affirmations stated just the way you want them, but keep at it until you have them letter-perfect. These affirmations can be written on scrap paper until you transfer them to your permanent notebook. Put each affirmation on a separate page. Read all of your affirmations at least three times a day, once in the morning after dressing, once in the afternoon, and once at night as you are in bed ready for sleep. Your affirmations should be the last thing your conscious mind thinks about before you fall asleep and the first thing your conscious mind thinks about when you awake.

Read each statement out loud, in a soft whisper or merely mouthed to yourself. Take notice of how you form the words, and see yourself doing and having the things which your affirmations declare. This is very important. You can pause after each affirmation; close your eyes and see yourself already in possession of your goal. You can see it, feel it, and act the part in your mind's eye.

Visualize and experience it as yours *now*. (Be like a child—that's the magic word!) There is one word that you must repeat over and over to yourself. This one word means success or failure in your quest for happiness and wealth. The absolutely imperative word is *visualization.*

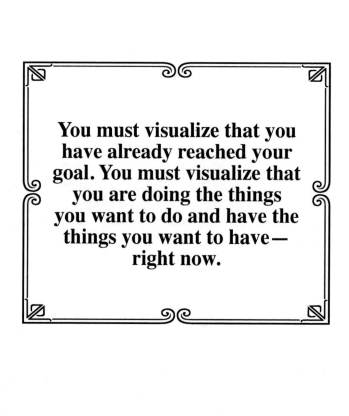

You must visualize that you have already reached your goal. You must visualize that you are doing the things you want to do and have the things you want to have—right now.

That's right, visualization! You must visualize that you have already reached your goal. I am not talking about day-dreaming! You must visualize that you are doing the things you want to do and have the things you want to have: right now.

The secret is to develop a feeling, and help it to form in your subconscious mind where you can act upon it. As the weeks and months pass, you will change your goals. Some you won't want, and these will be forgotten. Their pages in your notebook will be thrown away. You will set new goals as your excitement for happiness and wealth grows. You'll aim high, think big, and keep replacing your weaker goals with stronger, more meaningful ones.

It might seem silly to do this reading twice a day for weeks, month, and even years, but you are changing the habit patterns of your subconscious mind. You are changing deep-down negative thoughts, feelings, and fears. You have learned to say *no* to any thought about giving up this three-times-a-day-habit of reading and imprinting your affirmations. You can guarantee what you are reading will happen.

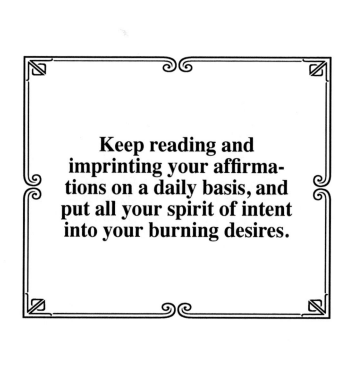

Keep reading and imprinting your affirmations on a daily basis, and put all your spirit of intent into your burning desires.

After you've been reading your success statements for four or five weeks, a thought will come to you that this is a silly gesture. After all, what would your friends think if they knew you were doing such a silly thing? The urge to quit will be strong, but your goal is a life of happiness and success, so you will stick with it and not give up. You will control and direct your negative self-talk.

As you continue your daily readings, visualization, experiencing and getting into action, you'll notice that you have a desire for one certain thing more than the others. This is your subconscious mind telling you to go after that goal first, where you are to put most of your energy and effort. This is the one thing which you think about twenty-four hours a day!

You put all your action, planning, and enthusiasm behind this goal, and set a date for its completion. It may be a long-range goal, or just one of the many, short steps to the big picture. Of course, you will not forget the other things you wrote down in your notebook. You will keep reading and imprinting your affirmations on a daily basis, and put all your spirit of intent into your burning desires.

Soon you will get ideas on what action to take. These ideas will come from the subconscious and should be acted upon. As these actions are taken, you will see yourself getting closer and closer to your goal. You'll finish that first goal and then move on to the next tangible goal. Remember, success is daily action towards the things you want next.

START IT NOW!

Notes:

Reflective Questions:
1. If time, money and circumstance were no problem what would you like to be, do, or have next?
2. Exactly what do you want?
3. What is your strongest desire?

Sample Affirmations:
- I know exactly what I want.
- I confidently expect to attain my number one goal.
- I have selected my number one goal, and I am taking action each day toward achieving it.
- I am focusing my energy and attention on my number one goal.

_____

_____

_____

_____

_____

_____

_____

_____

_____

_____

_____

_____

_____

_____

_____

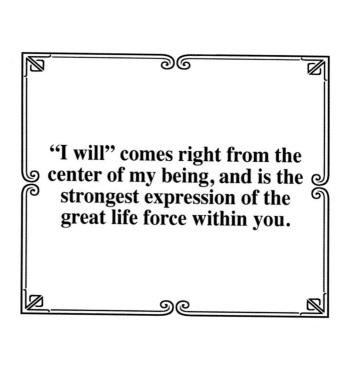

"I will" comes right from the center of my being, and is the strongest expression of the great life force within you.

Chapter 4: Strategy 3

How You Can Develop Persistence

T he shortest distance to happiness and wealth is through the habit of persistence. To reach your goal, your heart's desire, you must be persistent. If you do not succeed, you will try again. You never, ever give up!

Successful people are those who keep going when others have stopped. Willpower is the key to the door of success. Persistence is impossible without willpower. In every field of endeavor, the one predominant characteristic of success is an indomitable will.

The will can be made unconquerable through intelligent exercise and use.

The statement *I will* comes right from the center of my being, and is the strongest expression of the great life force within you.

You are a person of strong will, a positive, courageous, masterful individual in whom nature delights and rewards. The basis of all personal power resides in the will, and if you intend to accomplish anything in this world, you must acquire a powerful will. First comes self-belief in your abilities.

Then the will, with all the force, energy, and determination you can muster, becomes a dynamic force which sweeps away obstacles in its mighty onrush. Will is evidenced by persistence towards a goal.

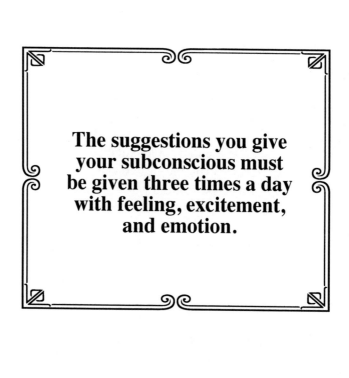

The suggestions you give
your subconscious must
be given three times a day
with feeling, excitement,
and emotion.

Persistence is *faith* in action. Every one of the Laws of Success must be applied with tenacity. These laws and concepts arise in the subconscious, and the best way to stimulate the subconscious is through repetition of success affirmations. The suggestions you give your subconscious must be given three times a day with feeling, excitement, and emotion. You must be centered on the habit of persisting with these goal affirmations and following up with action.

Your number one goal must be a burning desire. It must be the one thing you want more than anything else in the whole world. Think about it twenty-four hours a day. It's the first thing you think about in the morning and the last thing you think about at night.

Take your notebook with you as you crawl into bed every night. Have plenty of empty pages in your book to write down any ideas which might come to you during the night. Prop up the pillows and relax. Read your goal affirmations slowly and out loud. Pause after reading each affirmation and visualize that you are already in possession of that goal. You must have one specific, tangible goal: your foremost burning desire. Remember that concentration on one goal at a time will bring success.

After you have finished reading your affirmations and are ready to sleep, relax your body, close your eyes, and picture yourself living and enjoying your number one goal. See yourself doing the things you will be doing when your goal has been reached. Pretend that you have it now. Get emotional about it. Get the feeling that you already have your heart's desire. Go to sleep with this mental picture in your mind and the wonderful feeling of achieving the goal in your heart.

Play your affirmation audio while going to sleep.

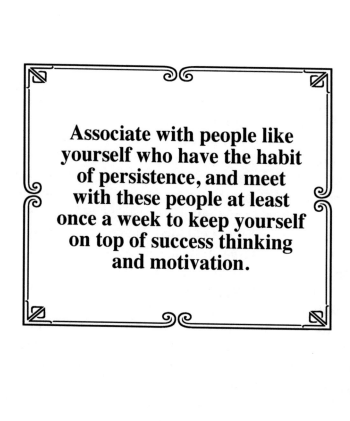

Associate with people like
yourself who have the habit
of persistence, and meet
with these people at least
once a week to keep yourself
on top of success thinking
and motivation.

Remember to get up early in the morning to have time for your hour of motivation and positive affirmations. Since you keep your notebook near your bed at night and in your office during the day, you see it and remember to read it throughout the day. Use several forms of reminders to make it easy for you to remember your daily readings. Write notes to yourself on your daily calendar pad, such as "read affirmations three times a day," and "get into action today!" Keep books on success and motivation near your bed, in your living room, and in your office. Keep a success-oriented book on the front seat of your car. Take an audio player or CDs with you and listen to audios on success and motivation each time you drive your car.

Repetition is the best way to form the habit of persistence, and to tap the subconscious mind for ideas. Read at least one chapter of a success book each day. Associate with people like yourself who have the habit of persistence, and meet with these people at least once a week to keep yourself on top of success thinking and motivation. Never put yourself down. Concentrate on one step at a time, and never, ever give up.

There must be energy in your resolution and grit in your determination in order to ultimately reach your goal. Realize that to succeed at anything of value requires tremendous resolution, vigorous self-faith, and steady, conscientious, whole hearted, unremitting *work!* Get busy and work with all your might.

There is no such thing as failure for the willing, ambitious, persistent worker. Know that the world steps aside for the determined and persistent person. Willpower makes a way, even through seemingly impossibilities.

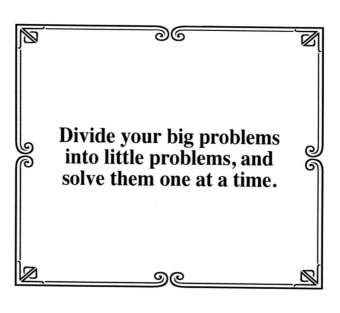

Divide your big problems
into little problems, and
solve them one at a time.

As an individual of intelligence, you have a definite schedule, and you have the willpower to follow it. Keep a fresh list of jobs to do, and then persistently do the thing that needs doing today. Make a definite decision to keep engagements on time. Start preparation early enough so that when the time comes to act, you'll be ready. Divide your big problems into little problems, and solve them one at a time.

Your will is strong and you thoroughly know beforehand what you are doing. Start unafraid, and persist through all obstacles to gain consistent victories and lay claim to your ultimate throne.

START IT NOW!

Notes:

Reflective Questions:
1. What actions are you going to take to increase your persistence?
2. How can you associate with people who have a habit of persistence?
3. What problem do you have that is blocking you from your number one goal?
4. How can you divide this problem up into smaller actionable steps that you can take?

Sample Affirmations:
- I focus on one goal at a time.
- I have a high level of indomitable will.
- I have the will to achieve my number one goal.
- I have a strong belief in myself.
- I associate with people that have a habit of persistence.

_____

_____

_____

_____

_____

_____

_____

_____

_____

_____

_____

_____

_____

_____

_____

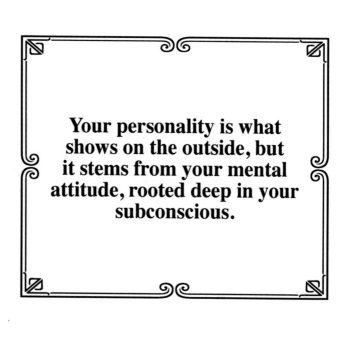

Your personality is what shows on the outside, but it stems from your mental attitude, rooted deep in your subconscious.

Chapter 5: Strategy 4

How to Develop the Proper Mental Attitude

T he proper mental attitude attracts more good and great things from life than the wrong one. If your thinking and your attitude are negative and you aren't receiving good and great things from life, you can change and adopt a positive attitude. When people look at you and listen to you, they see and hear your personality. Your personality is what shows on the outside, but it stems from your mental attitude, rooted deep in your subconscious.

The subconscious mind is a goal-striving, servomechanism, consisting of the brain, the heart, the nervous system, and the muscular system. All of these are used and directed by the mind (thoughts and beliefs), and the heart (feelings and emotions). Once properly programmed, this highly complex, creative mechanism will work automatically to achieve goals of success and happiness that you've set for it. As with any other servomechanism, it must have a clear-cut goal or objective. The goals that your creative mechanism seeks to achieve are images or mental pictures created through the use of your imagination.

The key goal image is your own self-image. Your creative mechanism makes use of stored information or memory in responding to current situations and solving problems. Your brain and nervous system function both as guidance systems, to automatically steer you in the right direction to achieve certain goals, and to give you needed answers, new ideas, and inspiration.

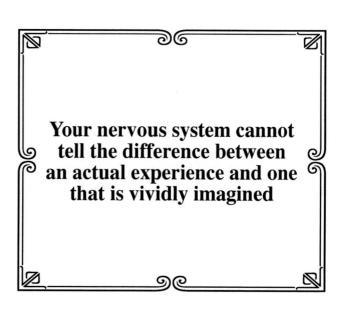

Your nervous system cannot tell the difference between an actual experience and one that is vividly imagined

This automatic creative mechanism within you can operate only if you provide the target. The realization that your actions, feelings, and behavior are the result of your own images and beliefs gives you the psychological leverage necessary for changing your attitude and self-image. Mental pictures offer you an opportunity to practice new traits and attitudes. This is possible because your nervous system cannot tell the difference between an actual experience and one that is vividly imagined. If you can picture yourself performing in a certain manner, to your mind, it's the same as the actual performance.

Attitude is your strongest habit. Formed early in life, it changes with your external environment, experience, and learning. Your past thoughts and years of life have created your present attitude. To purposefully change your attitude, you must change your thinking and habits of thought.

Reading your success affirmations three times a day will help to change your thought habits, and associating with positive, successful people will also help you to keep your thinking along the lines of the mental images you've determined necessary for your success and happiness. You'll begin to identify with and act like successful people.

The aim of self-image psychology is to find the real self and to bring a mental image of oneself more in line with the objects one represents. You must track down the belief about yourself, the world, or other people that are prompting your negative behavior. Does something always seem to happen to cause you to miss out, just as success seems within your grasp? Perhaps you secretly feel unworthy of success or believe that you don't deserve it. Both behavior and feelings spring from belief.

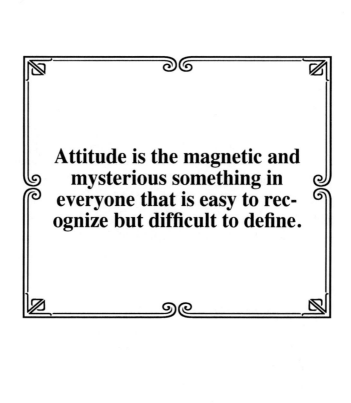

Attitude is the magnetic and mysterious something in everyone that is easy to recognize but difficult to define.

You must answer the following questions:

1. Are there any rational reasons for such a belief?
2. Could I be mistaken in this belief?
3. Would I come to the same conclusion about some other person in a similar situation?
4. And finally, should I continue to act and feel as if this were true if the belief is mistaken?

Attitude is the magnetic and mysterious something in everyone that is easy to recognize but difficult to define. It's the something to be released from within, and it's the outward evidence of the unique and individual creative self. This real self within every person is attractive, magnetic, and has a powerful impact and influence upon others. A positive attitude means that you've freed the creative potential within you, and that you're able to express your real self. There are many ways to develop and improve your self-image, and thereby your attitude and personality.

Read and study one personal effectiveness book per month. Think of yourself as being one of God's creatures, one of the greatest and most complex mechanisms in existence. Think about your number one goal as many times per day as you can. Picture your goal as being accomplished. Visualize that you already have it. You can see it, feel it, and experience it. Act like the person you want to be. If you act like a person with a positive attitude, that acting will make you a person with a positive attitude. It's that simple! Every time you think a positive thought, it helps to change the subconscious record that plays over and over throughout your life. Spaced repetition will change the message to one which says that you are successful, happy, and a great and wonderful person.

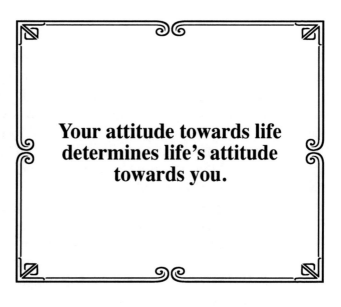

Your attitude towards life
determines life's attitude
towards you.

You are constantly thinking, yet you can only think one thought at a time. Each time you think a good, true, beautiful, and positive thought, it goes into your subconscious and helps to change your attitude from negative to positive. The person who keeps trying is happier than the person who doesn't try. Remember, your attitude towards life determines life's attitude towards you.

Positive attitudes produce positive results. Negative attitudes produce negative results.

It is very important that you read your success affirmations three times a day, especially those on your intangible goals. These are the personality changes that you are striving to accomplish. The affirmation exercises give you new habits of thought, and these become automatic reflexes of your subconscious mind. They replace the old habits of negative thinking, and soon you will act positively in every situation in life. Read this message over and over again, hundreds, even thousands of times, until your attitude becomes positive, excited, and good.

Here is an affirmation that can be repeated to help change thought habits from negative to positive: "I am filled with a positive mental attitude. I see only the good, the true, and the beautiful in all situations and people. I picture things as they should be. My imagination is full with positive ideas and pictures. I am a person who permits a situation to exist without judging it. I do not react emotionally to any negative situation or person."

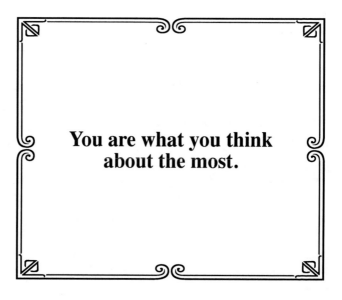

You are what you think
about the most.

You are what you think about the most. You have to develop in your subconscious a new and glamorous self-image, one that meets with yourself approval, as well as the picture of the person you truly aspire to be. By using affirmations and visualization, you can change your subconscious attitude and consequently your conscious attitude and behavior.

Your individual accomplishments are in direct proportion to your self-image. A healthy self-image is absolutely vital to your success. A poor self-image results in very little success. A beautiful, powerful self-image means tremendous success. An outstanding self-image equals a tremendously positive attitude.

START IT NOW!

Notes:

Reflective Questions:
1. What is your number one goal?
2. What is your mental attitude in regards to achieving your number one goal?
3. How can you use affirmations to align yourself image with your number one goal?
4. What is your attitude towards life?

Sample Affirmations:
- I have a positive mental attitude in regards to achieving my number one goal.
- I am empowered to take action toward my number one goal.
- I have a positive self image that is in alignment with achieving my number one goal.
- I have a positive attitude towards life and I feel great.

The way to be successful is to organize each day creatively, with time for study, thinking, planning, and action.

Chapter 6: Strategy 5

How to Organize Yourself and Your Time

If you cannot organize yourself and your time, you cannot succeed. The way to be successful and happy is to organize each day creatively, with time for study, thinking, planning, and action.

Each of your days is a total lifetime. You are reborn, you live, and you die each day. Start each day knowing that you are living your future today. Today is all there is. It is the ultimate trip.

You never feel anything, have anything, or do anything unless you feel it, act it, and do it now, today. So ask yourself repeatedly, "How can I best use this day? This hour? This minute?" This means planning your day and organizing your time.

The following tips will support you in organizing yourself and your time to achieve greater success:

- Make a list just before going to sleep at night. This list contains the six most important things that you have to do the next day, in order of your priority.
- Set aside a definite time each morning, and organize and plan the day by the hour. This is a breakdown of the list that was made the night before. You may also keep a copy of the list in your office and at home.

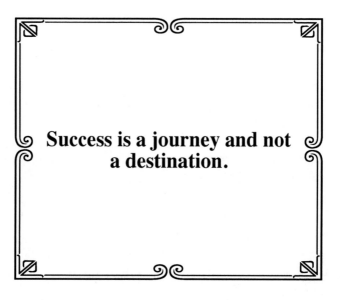

Success is a journey and not
a destination.

This is a plan of action that will direct you every hour of your productive day.

- Make every minute of your day count for something. Set aside at least one hour in the morning for goal and affirmation reading. Include your visualization time and time for some physical action on your tangible goal. Use some of the morning time for prayer and meditation. If you are working for someone else, plan your day so that a full day of achievement will be accomplished.
- Keep away from idle conversation.
- Plan your evenings so that you can get right to it after dinner. This is a good time to take action on your present goal. Make sure that not all of your time is spent on reading, studying, and visualizing. Learn to put most of your usable time into action on your immediate goal.
- Never look at success as a future possibility. It exists right now, today, this very minute! Success is a journey and not a destination. If you cannot be happy and successful today, you cannot be happy and successful tomorrow, for today is all there is! Remind yourself that success is achieved by taking daily action towards the things that you want next.

START IT NOW!

Notes

Reflective Questions:
1. How can you best use today?
2. How can you best use this week?
3. How can you best use this month?
4. What is your plan of action for the month?

Sample Affirmations:
- I plan my day and I organize my time before I go to sleep.
- I make a list of the six most important things I have to do each day, and I do them with passion.
- I take consistent action on my immediate goal.
- I am happy and successful today.
- Start it now!

_____

_____

_____

_____

_____

_____

_____

_____

_____

_____

_____

_____

_____

_____

_____

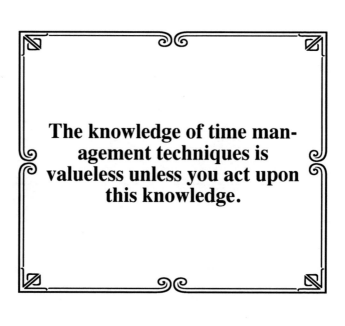

The knowledge of time management techniques is valueless unless you act upon this knowledge.

Time Management

The management of time is probably the most important action a person can take to improve his or her efficiency in achieving goals. Very few people have mastered that one precious commodity: *time*.

Hundreds of books and articles on time management are available. Each of them offers many concrete suggestions on how to get more done in less time and with improved efficiency. Much of this advice is good; most of this advice will work if people actually follow it.

A time management technique that is easy to follow and can result in a dramatic improvement in efficiency is the establishment of short-range goals within a priority system.

One word of warning, however: regardless of how much you know about how to manage time, the knowledge is of little value unless you exercise it. Just as a person should not be paid for what they know but for what they accomplish, the knowledge of time management techniques is valueless unless you act upon this knowledge. You can know all the techniques of better time management and yet never seem to have time to do all the things that must be done. The technique of listing the things which need to be done and assigning priorities to them is fine, but the act of writing them down won't do the job by itself. You have to take the initiative and actually accomplish the things you have listed, or at least attempt to accomplish them. And in reality, between twenty-five to fifty percent of people report feeling overwhelmed or *burned out at work*.

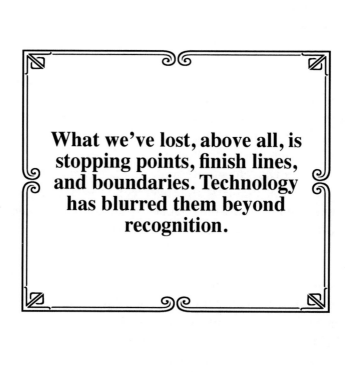

What we've lost, above all, is stopping points, finish lines, and boundaries. Technology has blurred them beyond recognition.

It's not just the number of hours we're working, but also the fact that we spend too many continuous hours juggling too many things at the same time.

What we've lost, above all, is stopping points, finish lines, and boundaries. Technology has blurred them beyond recognition. Wherever we go, our work follows us on our digital devices, ever insistent and intrusive. It's like an itch we can't resist scratching, even though scratching invariably makes it worse.

Tell the truth: Do you answer email during conference calls (and sometimes even during calls with one other person)? Do you bring your laptop to meetings and then pretend you're taking notes while you surf the net? Do you eat lunch at your desk? Do you make calls while you're driving and even send the occasional text, even though you know you shouldn't?

The biggest cost—assuming you don't crash—is to your productivity. In part, that's a simple consequence of splitting your attention, so that you're partially engaged in multiple activities but rarely fully engaged in any one of them. In part, it's because when you switch away from a primary task to do something else, you're *increasing the time* it takes to finish that task by an average of twenty-five percent.

But most insidiously, if you're always doing something, you're relentlessly burning down your available *reservoir of energy* over the course of every day, and therefore you have less available energy with every passing hour.

The best way for an organization to fuel higher productivity and more innovative thinking is to strongly encourage finite periods of absorbed focus, as well as shorter periods of real renewal.

Stop demanding or expecting instant responsiveness at every moment of the day.

If you're a manager, here are three policies worth promoting:

1. **Maintain meeting discipline.** Schedule meetings for forty-five minutes, rather than an hour or longer, so participants can stay focused. Take time afterward to reflect on what's been discussed, and recover before the next obligation. Start all meetings at a precise time, end at a precise time, and insist that all digital devices be turned off throughout the meeting.

2. **Stop demanding or expecting instant responsiveness at every moment of the day.** It forces your people into reactive mode, fractures their attention, and makes it difficult for them to sustain attention on their priorities. Let them turn off their email at certain times. If it's urgent, you can call them—but that won't happen very often.

3. **Encourage renewal.** Create at least one time during the day when you encourage your people to stop working and take a break. Offer a mid-afternoon class in yoga, or meditation, organize a group walk or workout, or consider creating a renewal room where people can relax, or take a nap.

It's also up to individuals to set their own boundaries. Consider these three behaviors for yourself:

1. **Do the most important thing first in the morning**, preferably without interruption, for sixty to ninety minutes, with a clear starting and stopping time. If possible, work in a private space during this period, or with sound-reducing earphones. Finally, resist every impulse to distraction, knowing that you have a designated stopping point. The more absorbed you can get, the more productive you'll be. When you're done, take at least a few minutes to renew.

When you're engaged at work, fully engage, for defined periods of time. When you're renewing, truly renew.

2. **Establish regular, scheduled times to think more long term, creatively, or strategically**. If you don't, you'll constantly succumb to the tyranny of the urgent. Also, find a different environment in which to do this activity — preferably one that's relaxed and conducive to open-ended thinking.

3. **Take real and regular vacations**. Real means that when you're off, you're truly disconnecting from work. Regular means several times a year if possible, even if some are only two or three days added to a weekend. The research strongly suggests that you'll be far healthier and more productive overall if you *take all of your vacation time*.

A single principle lies at the heart of all these suggestions. When you're engaged at work, fully engage, for defined periods of time. When you're renewing, truly renew. Make waves. Stop living your life in the gray zone.

Always remember that there is no short cut to time management. You have to want to do it, learn how, then actually practice it and then time becomes your ally and not an enemy. Try it . . . it works!

START IT NOW!

Notes:

Reflective Questions
1. What are your short-range goals and their priority?
2. How can you use more of your time management knowledge?
3. What are your most important goals for this month?
4. What actions are you going to take in regards to your most important goals this month?

Sample Affirmations?
- I have established my short-range goals and their priorities.
- Time is my ally and it helps me achieve my number one goal faster.
- Each day I set clear starting and stopping points.
- I focus on completing one thing at a time.

_____

_____

_____

_____

_____

_____

_____

_____

_____

_____

_____

_____

_____

_____

_____

_____

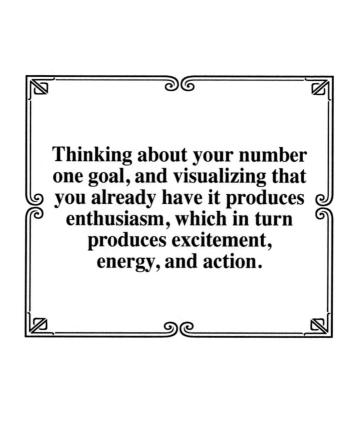

Thinking about your number
one goal, and visualizing that
you already have it produces
enthusiasm, which in turn
produces excitement,
energy, and action.

How to Become Enthusiastic and Why

Y ou can have whatever you want as fast as you want it if you get excited and enthused about having it. Thinking about your number one goal, and visualizing that you already have it produces enthusiasm, which in turn produces excitement, energy, and action.

The subconscious is stimulated by excitement. Enthusiasm steps up the vibration of the mind and the heart. If you act enthusiastically, you will be enthusiastic.

Here is how to get excited and enthused. Get up an hour earlier in the morning than your usual time. As you spend thirty minutes or more in the bathroom, smile every time you see your reflection in the mirror. Look at yourself and smile. Say out loud to yourself, "I feel great! This is a fantastic day! Today I will think about my number one goal as many times as I can." Brush your teeth vigorously and imagine that your mind is as alert and stimulated as your mouth and teeth are clean and fresh.

With your now clean, fresh mind, visualize that you already have your goal. Think it, feel it, and visualize that its yours right now. You can visualize that you're on a stage, acting out the part before a thousand people. Do not say, "But I don't feel excited. I'm sleepy; I'm tired." If you feel that way it's because you are thinking that way. The way to change your thinking and feeling is to act the positive part.

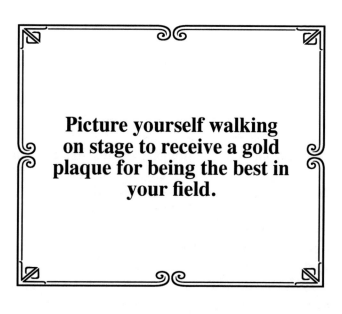

Picture yourself walking on stage to receive a gold plaque for being the best in your field.

Act happy to become happy. Act enthusiastically to become enthused.

Try it right now. Say to yourself, "I act enthusiastically and I feel enthused." Say it out loud three times. Then say, "I feel great, everyone feels great—the whole world feels great. Life is wonderful."

After leaving the bathroom, sit down and relax. Take your affirmation book and spend the next thirty minutes reading over your list, and again visualize that you already have your goals. All your goals are yours right now. It's a wonderful feeling. Picture yourself being congratulated by your friends. Picture yourself walking on stage to receive a gold plaque for being the best in your field. Picture your huge sums of money safely tucked away in a large bank vault. Picture yourself being escorted into the vault by the bank president. Picture yourself touching all your money. Say out loud to yourself, "I am great. I am very happy, and I am very wealthy."

Now relax and spend a few minutes thinking about your number one goal, the one for which you have a set time limit, the one goal which you will reach before progressing on to the others. The next step is a very important one: write down all the "how-to" ideas in regards to your goal that come to you and then integrate them into your critical action plan for implementation.

START IT NOW!

Notes:

Reflective Questions:
1. How can you use affirmations to help you become enthusiastic about you number one goal?
2. How can you use visualization to become enthusiastic about your number one goal?
3. What actions can you take to achieve your number one goal?

Sample Affirmations:
- I feel enthusiastic and I feel enthused.
- I feel great.
- I feel alive.
- I am enthusiastic about my number one goal.

Your great achievements
will come when you do not
adjust to other people and
their opinions.

Chapter 8: Strategy 7

How to Be Yourself

You are unique. You are the only one of you in the world of seven billion souls. If you will show your individuality, the world will push you to success.

Yet ninety percent of the people in this country are not finding the success, happiness, and wealth they want. The reason for this failure is that everyone is acting like everyone else. We are a society of copycats. We conform to the way we think other people want us to act. Many of us are afraid to go out on our own and to act like ourselves: to be individuals.

The thing that will keep you successful and happy is being an individual, being yourself. God made the original when he made you. You will do things in your lifetime that no other person has ever done, and no other person will ever do again. Your great achievements will come when you do not adjust to other people and their opinions.

Always remember that you have the power, the ability, and the right to look any person in the eye and say, "No, thank you." Failure, frustration, and mental illness can come if we try to live up to the standards, opinions, and thoughts of someone else. Your opinion is as important, if not more important than any others. You should strive to build a better you. Be the best you, you can be. Being an individual does not mean being the same personality throughout life. True individuality takes time to develop and grow. You will be improving yourself throughout your entire life. Many of us have spent a lifetime copying others.

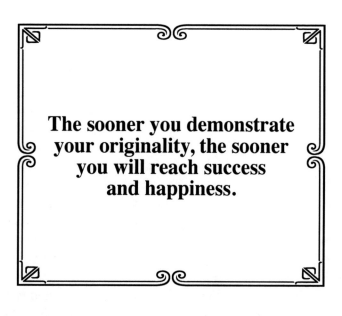

The sooner you demonstrate
your originality, the sooner
you will reach success
and happiness.

Remember that you are a unique original, and that you should never try to be exactly like anyone else.

Look to someone you admire or who has done particularly well in your area of interest for someone to model yourself after during the time you're developing your own particular talents and abilities. You do not live another's life. You live your own life. It is also advisable to read and study the lives of great men and women to gain insight into how they used their own uniqueness to win great victories of wealth, happiness, and success.

Being an individual means becoming what you want to be and what you need to be. The sooner you demonstrate your originality, the sooner you will reach success and happiness. If you are not doing the work you enjoy doing, start doing the work you love to do on the side.

By all means you should keep your present job, but, for instance, you could turn your garage into a place of business or build a workshop in the backyard to begin working on your dreams. You may take an online training program to learn more about your burning desire.

If you have an urge to do something else, that's your individuality trying to come to the front. Recognize it, and let it go at that. Don't play games with other people's minds. Be straightforward and honest. It's great when others understand you because it means they're experiencing your internal spirit of intent. If they don't and they get hurt as a result, that's their problem.

Make sure that your spirit of intent is aligned with your actions. Associate only with positive, considerate, dynamic people.

A good attitude is infectious. If you associate with people who live life to the utmost every minute, you will both benefit and be reinforced. You decide who you want to be; then give it every ounce of love you can find. You will be you, happy and wealthy.

START IT NOW!

Notes

Reflective Questions
1. Who are some of the great people that you can read about to gain insights in regards to how they used their uniqueness?
2. What can you do to build a better you?
3. How can you associate with positive, considerate, and dynamic people more?
4. How can you develop your individuality?

Sample Affirmations:
- I am a unique original.
- I am an individual.
- My opinion is important.
- I am building a better me.
- My spirit and intent is in alignment with my number one goal.

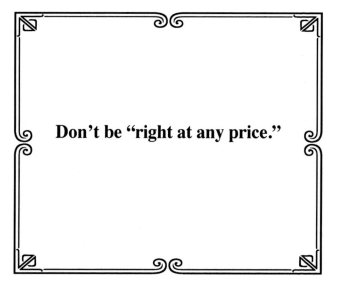

Don't be "right at any price."

Chapter 9: Strategy 8

How to Sell Yourself

I t's not what you know that counts, but how you act upon it by selling yourself to others. The finest art is that of selling oneself to others. Every action you take, every word you say, every thought you think goes out to others, and comes back in the same manner in which it was given. This is no great secret, but it *is* the law of action and reaction. If you love and serve other people, other people will love and serve you.

Selling yourself is a matter of being thoughtful and following several proven rules or principles of those who have achieved wealth and happiness.

One very important rule is this: Don't be "right at any price." Let the other person be right. When you understand your principles, there is no conflict. By their set of values, they are right, and you gain—not lose—by allowing that to be.

Here are the principles you should memorize and use constantly:

- Be observant of the good people do, and praise them for it.
- Be a positive wizard.
- Encourage people to attempt great things.
- Never intentionally embarrass a person.
- Ask polite questions instead of telling a person what to do.
- Have the attitude of, "How can I support the other

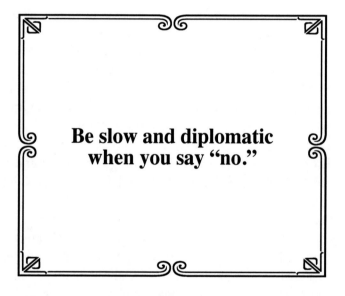

**Be slow and diplomatic
when you say "no."**

person *(help find the pay-value for them)?*"

- Encourage the other person to do most of the talking.
- Help the other person to think and speak in positive ways.
- When you are wrong, say so, before the other person does.
- Don't come right out and tell the other person they are wrong.
- Help them visualize what it would be like without the problem.
- Don't argue, but build up the other person's importance.
- Learn to listen more than you talk.
- Use the other person's name often in conversation.
- Do a lot of smiling and whistling and singing. (People like to be around a happy person!)
- Show an interest in people.
- Do not tease and joke with people because it does not make friends.
- Look for the good in people in all situations.
- Constantly think of ways to make people happy.

One does not have to be a meek, milquetoast, yes-person, but if you want to sell yourself, learn how to say "Yes!" quickly and enthusiastically. Be slow and diplomatic when you say "no." In most situations a no can be said with thoughtfulness and politeness. It is not the no you say, but the way in which you say it that will be remembered. You have the power, the ability, and the right to look a person in the eyes and say, "No, thank you."

Here is an affirmation that will help with human relations: "I am a good and thoughtful person. I am thoughtful of other people's feelings. I see the good in others."

START IT NOW!

Notes

Reflective Questions:
1. What are the behaviors that support you in selling yourself?
2. What are the behaviors that negatively impact your ability to sell yourself?
3. What actions can you take to increase your effectiveness in regards to selling yourself?

Sample Affirmations:
- I am a very positive wizard to others.
- I am masterful at asking polite questions that build trust and respect.
- I have a positive attitude of "how can I support you in getting what you want."

_____

_____

_____

_____

_____

_____

_____

_____

_____

_____

_____

_____

_____

_____

_____

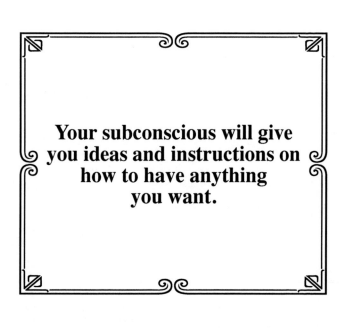

Your subconscious will give
you ideas and instructions on
how to have anything
you want.

How to Use Your Imagination For Wealth and Happiness

You can achieve whatever you create in your imagination. Your greatest power is that of thought. Through your ability to think, you can use your imagination to create mental pictures, which can be either positive or negative. You are not interested in negative mental pictures because they can be damaging to your mental, physical, and spiritual being.

You are only interested in positive imagination, the kind which will help you to achieve whatever you want in life. Yes, you can have anything which your imagination can conceive, when you really want it, when it is really right for you, and when you believe with every cell in your body that you can have it.

What you need to do is to learn techniques that will bring together the conscious, subconscious, and creative subconscious functioning powers of your mind. With these powers of your mind working together on one tangible goal, you know it is just a matter of time until you reach that goal. Your subconscious will give you ideas and instructions on how to have anything you want.

All you have to do is feed it information, ask questions, and be prepared for the answers.

Your imagination is part of your conscious thinking. You can imagine anything you want. You can do and be anything

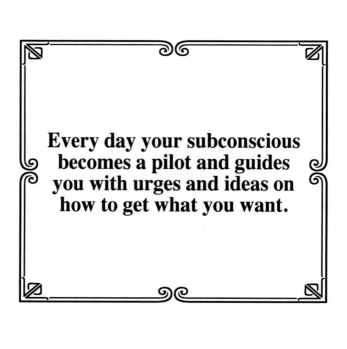

Every day your subconscious becomes a pilot and guides you with urges and ideas on how to get what you want.

and everything in your conscious imagination. The secret is to believe what you imagine. When you think, feel, and act as though something is true, that believability goes into your subconscious, which accepts it and responds by providing you with ideas on how to do it even better.

Every day your subconscious becomes a pilot and guides you with urges and ideas on how to get what you want.

Here are some techniques, which can help the imagination to create better images, and in turn help to generate ideas, enthusiasm, and action: a loose-leaf notebook is a must, and within it are your tangible and intangible goals, written as strong and positive statements in the present tense. You can transfer your statements to your electronic device later for easier use. These statements must be read at least three times a day, accompanied by visualizing that the goals are yours right now, this very minute.

Find someone to take a picture of you with your number one goal. If the goal is a new car, go to the showroom and ask the dealer to allow you to have your photo taken with the exact model and color you want. If your goal is a new home, search until you have found one that is similar to the one that you want. Tell the owner what you're doing, and why, and ask if you might have your picture taken (with your family, if you like) in front of the house.

If your goal is to become a surgeon, ask a surgeon to loan you an operating room gown and a few instruments for the picture. If your goal is to pilot your own airplane, have your picture taken with you at the controls. Try to get the feelings you'll have when you've achieved your goals. The more feelings you get from these games of visualization, the better it will be for your subconscious. What is gained through these games of visualization? An excitement and enthusiasm for your goals and a strong desire to take action. When you get excited, your whole body, soul, and creative mind are working together to bring you to your goal as soon

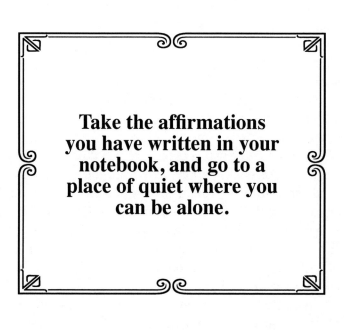

Take the affirmations
you have written in your
notebook, and go to a
place of quiet where you
can be alone.

as possible. Remember, success is the doing and the being and has very little to do with the future.

Another effective technique in stirring the imagination is to make your own success audio. Take the affirmations you have written in your notebook, and go to a place of quiet where you can be alone.

In a relaxed voice, read your affirmations out loud with as much feeling as you can muster. When this is done, you will have created your own success audio recording. This audio should be played as many times as convenient. Play the audio at work, in your car, or around the house while doing your weekend chores. Another very effective way to use this audio is to play it as you are falling asleep at night.

Invest in a good audio player with an automatic shut off feature, and after the lights are out and you've crawled into bed, turn the player on and listen to your audio recording. Lie back and relax your entire body. As you sleep, the success statements are going into your subconscious.

When the audio is over and you're sound asleep, the player will shut itself off automatically. Your subconscious mind will think about your goals while you sleep. During that time, your mind will be searching, planning, and finding better ideas on how to reach your goals. Keep a notebook and pencil at your bedside. Some ideas will be so powerful that they will actually awaken you. Write them down before you fall back to sleep.

The first couple of hours in the morning are the most productive. This is the time when you may get your most creative ideas. You can achieve what you imagine.

START IT NOW!

Notes:

Reflective Questions
1. How can you use mental pictures to create your goals?
2. How can your imagination support you in achieving your goals?
3. What do you want to be, do, or have?
4. What are your top tangible and intangible goals?

Sample Affirmations:
- I am wealthy and successful.
- I am happy and fulfilled.
- I take care of my physical body and it is healthy.
- My mind, body, and spirit are well balanced and in harmony.

_____

_____

_____

_____

_____

_____

_____

_____

_____

_____

_____

_____

_____

_____

_____

_____

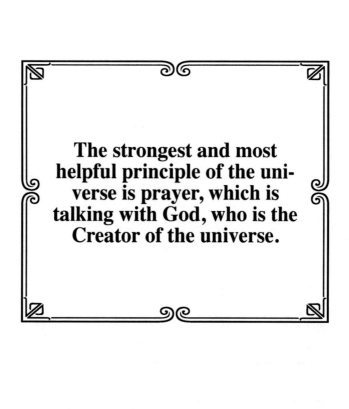

The strongest and most helpful principle of the universe is prayer, which is talking with God, who is the Creator of the universe.

How to Break Nonproductive Habits

There is a guaranteed way to rid yourself of nonproductive habits and replace them with productive ones. Normally, a human being cannot break a strong habit without outside help.

There is a Universal Power greater than you, which you can call upon for help. Tapping the source of this Power can release your limitless power for happiness and wealth.

The strongest and most helpful principle of the universe is prayer, which istalking with God, who is the Creator of the universe and who is very close to us. You can't see or touch God, but you can believe that God is a part of every cell in your body. Your contact with God is the strongest force in the world.

All things are possible through God. When you pray, God hears you. You can see, hear, and feel God receiving your prayers. The best conditions for prayer are when you are alone and all is quiet. The prayer conversation should be between you and God only. No one else can hear God speak to you because you have an individual relationship with God.

All things are possible through God. You can stop any nonproductive habit. You can begin any good habit, find a purpose for living, amass great wealth, become happy and prosperous, and make the world a better place for all, with God's help.

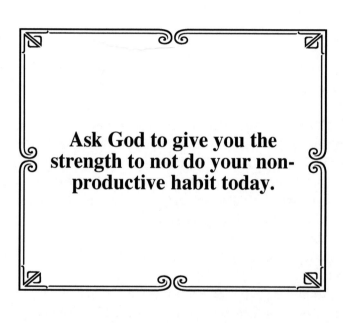

Ask God to give you the
strength to not do your nonproductive habit today.

You probably have some habits which you would like to change or stop. Here's an excellent method of stopping those habits:

The first thing to do is ask: "Do I really want to break this habit?" There must be a deep inner feeling and knowledge that this is a habit which you really want to break; that it is a habit which hinders your success and consumes your precious time, energy, and money.

The next step is very, very important. Ask your religious leader or a very close and trusted friend to pray for you and ask God to help you break your nonproductive or negative habit. The person praying for you should be praying on the same day on which you do your praying.

It does not have to be together or at the same church, but there is a great deal of power generated when two minds pray on the same day on the same subject and to the same heavenly Father. God can make it quick and easy for you to break any nonproductive habit!

The next step must be done every morning without fail. It is an important part of the prayer. Thank God for helping you. Pray in a manner which makes you feel closer to God, and be certain that you thank God for helping you to avoid your nonproductive habit yesterday. Then ask God to give you the strength to not do your habit today.

Talking with God in this way and asking for His help will provide you with a willpower so strong that you *will* yourself not to do your nonproductive habit on the day of your prayer. Soon that habit will be forgotten. The nonproductive habit will have been replaced by a positive habit, one of asking for and receiving help from God in not doing the unwanted behavior. This new, positive habit will have replaced the old, nonproductive habit in your subconscious.

When you are over the negative habit, you can go on to another friend, another day of mutual prayer, and daily talk with God.

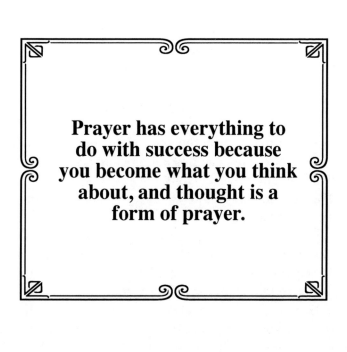

Prayer has everything to do with success because you become what you think about, and thought is a form of prayer.

That's how negative or nonproductive habits can be broken. If the habits ever return, use prayer and God's help to banish them again.

Prayer is a power that never fails. Prayer has everything to do with success because you become what you think about, and thought is a form of prayer. God knows the instant you think a thought. Every thought you have throughout your entire lifetime is a thought with God.

Reading your success affirmations three times a day is similar to praying, and this is why it is so important to start your readings with a prayer. Your prayer could be similar to this: "Dear God, thank You for this wonderful day and the great opportunities it holds for me. As I read my affirmations, I know they're entering into my subconscious, and You are hearing and acting on them. Thank You, God, for helping me to achieve my number one goal."

No one knows all of the hidden and secret powers of the universe, but we do know, or believe, that there is someone, something, or some power far greater than us, and there are times in our lives when we need this power.

The need for creative power should never leave your subconscious. It should be with you twenty-four hours a day. You can help your subconscious find the answers to your individual goals and desires by consciously thinking and praying about your next goal as often as you can and by reading your affirmations three times a day without fail. Our Great Creator does not play favorites between his mortal children here on Earth, but He does endow us each with three powers. Using these three powers, you can be anything you want to be and have anything you want to have.

These three powers are:

    Thought,

        Choice,

            and Prayer.

            START IT NOW!

Notes:

Reflective Questions:
1. What are your nonproductive habits?
2. Which nonproductive habits do you want to break?
3. How can you use God to help you break your nonproductive habits?
4. How can you use prayer to break your nonproductive habits?

Sample Affirmations:
- I am productive.
- I have developed the habit of being productive
- Thank you God for this wonderful day and the great opportunities it holds for me.
- Thank you God for helping me achieve my number one goal.
- Thank you God for helping me be productive.

_____

_____

_____

_____

_____

_____

_____

_____

_____

_____

_____

_____

_____

_____

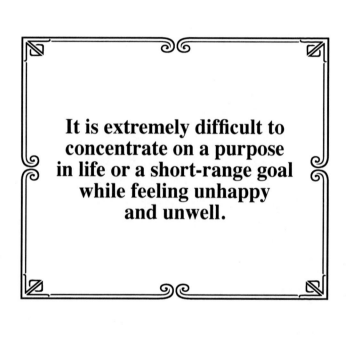

It is extremely difficult to concentrate on a purpose in life or a short-range goal while feeling unhappy and unwell.

How to Be Healthy

Y ou must get into good physical shape and stay healthy if you want to be happy and wealthy. Some people are fortunate enough to be born with perfect health and maintain it all of their lives, while others have to work hard at getting into shape and good health. No matter which group you may fall into, it's your duty to live as long as you can. You must accomplish great things for yourself, your family, and mankind. Rest assured, you were put on this Earth for a reason, and you have a purpose for living. To discover that purpose or niche in your life, you must remain in good health, with excitement and zest for living. If you have to worry and fret about your health every day, if you feel sickly, weak, and unable to take another step, it's not likely that you'll be thinking very much about success.

Not all sick people are failures, but it is extremely difficult to concentrate on a purpose in life or a short-range goal while feeling unhappy and unwell. Healthy people are generally happy people. When you feel "on top of the world"— you *are* "on top of the world!"

Wish yourself a "Happy Birthday" by getting a complete physical exam each year. It's a good healthy habit and a great birthday present to yourself. Before you go to bed tonight, mark your birthday on the calendar with a big, red circle and the words, "get a physical." The biggest benefit of a physical exam may be a psychological boost because it will make you think, act, and feel better about yourself. When the doctor

Don't try to perform strenuous workout or exercises until you have a plan approved by your doctor.

says that everything's okay and you're in great shape, you'll feel like running down the steps instead of taking the elevator. You'll feel like clicking your heels and singing as you walk briskly to your car.

What can you do to get into shape, and better still, what can you do to stay in shape? The first thing is to visit a local health food store. Meet the manager and explain that you want to buy the store's very best book on health. Tell them that you want to go on a health kick and ask that they suggest the best vitamins and minerals for you.

To get started, read the health book you purchased, do some meditating, and pray for God's help. (Remember, the strongest principle in the universe is prayer.) Don't try to perform strenuous workout or exercises until you have a plan approved by your doctor. Make a commitment to cut way down on salt, sugar, and eliminate any fast foods. Reduce or eliminate your drinking of coffee or tea; the caffeine is harmful to the heart and nervous system. Nicotine and alcohol are both killers if not used in moderation, and should be avoided if possible.

"Moderation in everything" is a good rule to follow, for your health as well. As long as *you* are in control, everything will be fine. Another suggestion for better health and longer life is to do some form of physical exercise each day. Fast walking is an excellent form of exercise that can be performed by almost everyone. Exercise does not have to be hard work to be effective.

Get essential proteins every day, but only in moderate amounts. If you want to be happy and wealthy and live the life of success, you must use more and more of your brain power, talents, and abilities. You cannot do this with dull, dreary, half-dead brain cells. Form good health habits and make a point of taking care of yourself.

Most of us are weak in the willpower department. Our old habit patterns are cut so deeply into our subconscious

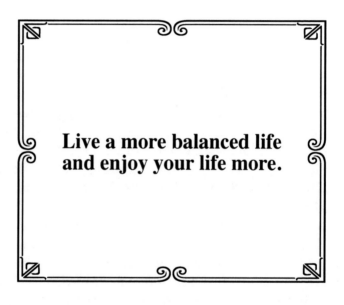

Live a more balanced life
and enjoy your life more.

that we do negative things almost automatically. But when you follow the Pragmatic Strategies for Success in your daily life, you'll:

- Become ten times more enthusiastic about your goals,
- Utilize good human relations skills,
- Become a person of action,
- Achieve your goals faster, and
- Live a more balanced life and enjoy your life more.

You'll call upon the great power of prayer. You'll become tenacious and never give up. You'll use your imagination, keep a proper mental attitude and be true to yourself. You'll organize your time. You'll get into healthy shape and stay that way.

In short, you'll improve your mental, physical, and spiritual aspects, and by doing so, you'll put yourself firmly on the journey to success and happiness.

START IT NOW!

Notes

Reflective Questions
1. What is your purpose—the reason for your life?
2. What are you unhappy about?
3. What are you going to do about the things that you are not happy about?
4. What do you need to stop, start, or continue doing to be healthier?

Sample Affirmations:
- I am healthy and happy.
- I am taking care of my body.
- I eat right and exercise daily.
- I have a positive mental attitude.

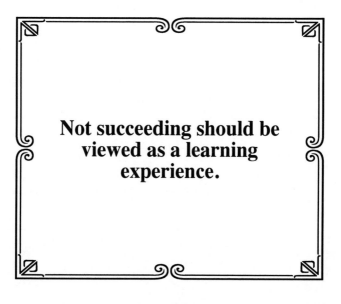

Not succeeding should be viewed as a learning experience.

How to Bounce Back
from a Setback

Y our ability to succeed is directly proportional to your ability to NOT SUCCEED. You must be able to attempt and not succeed, or you may never succeed.

The desire to grow is frustrated by the fear of not succeeding, or failing. Not succeeding should be viewed as a learning experience. Analyze what went wrong with your efforts and what went right. Try again by doing the right things correctly and by correcting those things that went wrong. If you really want to do that thing and if you objectively analyze and correct the errors, you will succeed.

The role of evaluation in achieving success is poorly understood by most people. We tend to blame ourselves for a poor performance, rather than to evaluate the performance in terms of its effectiveness in reaching the goal we have set. This is when "scientific objectivity" plays its major part.

A bowler, for example, cannot allow himself to indulge in self-hatred or recriminations if his ball has failed to carry a strike. The serious bowler will examine his actions, how the ball was rolled, the line it took to the pins, and so on.

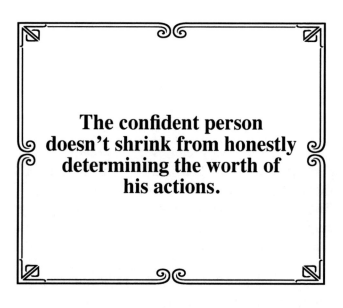

The confident person
doesn't shrink from honestly
determining the worth of
his actions.

Then he'll attempt to make the necessary corrections in the next frame.

It may take several frames for the adjustments to become fine tuned and effective, but those frames have been learning experiences, and have provided valuable information and feedback on the bowler's technique. By viewing those nonstrike frames in a negative manner, and by denying himself the value of the input, the bowler can only depend on luck to alter his game. If the nonstrike frames are viewed from a positive perspective, then it becomes a learning experience, and the bowler can use the information on what went wrong to make corrections and generally improve his game.

This is true of almost all sports activities, and this difference in attitudes and perceptions can spell a gradual improvement in some player, while others, through refusing to view failure as a learning experience, will remain poor or mediocre players for as long as they participate in the game.

The confident person doesn't shrink from honestly determining the worth of his actions. He isn't crushed if his evaluation shows that he has made a mistake or even if it shows that his ideas were completely wrong.

On the contrary, he is glad to learn what the failure has to teach him. He can now determine how to come closer to his goal on the next attempt. The chief roadblock to positive achievement is not failure, but *fear of failure*. We are afraid of what we do not know or of what we misunderstand. *Unreasonable fear is the enemy of effective action*.

The decision to succeed is a very personal one. A person can remain a mediocre, low income, low happiness individual and adjust to the unrewarding mess of his life by crying and suffering in misery and self-pity. But adjusting to misery is not sufficient or rewarding. Life is too short and too precious to choose such a fate.

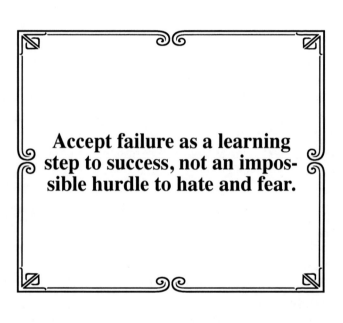

Accept failure as a learning step to success, not an impossible hurdle to hate and fear.

The alternative is to accept failure as a learning step to success, not an impossible hurdle to hate and fear.

Mental illness can develop when the desire to grow is frustrated by the fear of failing. One can become mired in misery and defeat. Part of the frustration can be removed if one is able to determine the cause of the fear. To overcome your difficulty in handling failure, successfully deal with it by learning the nature of motivation.

When your basic needs are understood, you'll understand what motivates you. You set goals only because your needs demand to be satisfied. Your needs generate desire within you, and the desire serves to motivate you towards your goal. A goal is simply an extension of a need. If you achieve the goal, you satisfy the need. Understanding your needs will dramatize any fear of failure which you may be experiencing.

Make a list of what you believe to be your six most basic needs, beginning with the most important. To help, visualize yourself on a desert island. What would be your greatest concern? Your next greatest?

At the core your basic needs are food, clothing, and shelter, another, security, which in today's society is usually measured by money. Money cannot assure happiness. However if one of your goals is to achieve material success then a strong drive will allow you to overcome setbacks and follow that goal through to completion.

What would you want to accomplish in your life if you could do whatever you wanted without restrictions? Make a list, and it will help you recognize the needs which might be driving you, and could include success, recognition, some physical or sport activity, financial attainment, family needs, or more personal ones. Your needs might include self-acceptance—by itself, it is potentially one of the most powerful *or* destructive needs.

Your ability to become successful depends on the degree of your self-acceptance, which is based on *your* success patterns.

When we stop trying,
we stop achieving.

Your patterns will determine if you have the stamina to try and not succeed, but still continue trying. There is a breaking point for every individual. There is only a finite amount of failure an individual can handle before wanting to quit. When we stop trying, we stop achieving.

Most people are not prepared for risk situations. They may have been protected from failure, conditioned not only through school experiences but also by their parents, with the admonition, "Be popular. Be accepted. Fit in. Be nice. Don't fail. Adjust." The real challenge is to determine the best way to take command, rather than deferring to the easiest alternative and seeking protection. If the desire for achievement is checked by fear of failure, you will be blocked from your goals, but more importantly, you will be blocked from knowing the causes of the problem.

Make a list of those experiences you find most threatening, such as selling a new product, getting a better job, starting your own business, and so forth. Determine what you believe to be the cause of your fears. Once you understand the nature of your fears, you can establish the action to be taken in removing them. One of man's basic needs is to be in a state of equilibrium, to be comfortable, to avoid anxiety. Man has a split personality, two voices within him coming from the positive self-image and the negative self-image. Ask yourself about something you have failed at before, but are about to try again.

What does your negative self-image say to you? "You can't do it. You've failed before. Remember what happened last time." What does your positive self-image say to you? "Well, let's try it one more time! Maybe we can do it this time." If you try and fail once more, your negative self-image will tell you, "I told you so. Why did you bother trying at all?" Hopefully, your positive self-image would tell you, "At least we tried. We got closer than last time. Maybe next time."

The appreciation of your potential will have a dramatic impact on the way you handle success.

If you try and succeed, your negative self-image may tell you, "You're lucky, and you'd better quit while you're ahead!" Your positive self-image will be excited by the success, and will be telling you, "Let's do it again! We can make it two in a row!"

This internal conflict between the negative and positive self-images can cause anxiety and destroy your basic need to be in equilibrium. It can cause an internal argument that can motivate you to avoid change and to remain in a state of equilibrium. To change requires that you become your own teacher, parent, or manager. You need to manage yourself, and this often means forcing yourself into success patterns. You need to make yourself change.

To do this requires that you first appreciate your potential. If you do this but do not succeed, you will realize that something went wrong because you deserve to succeed. You'll have to try again twice as hard next time or try a step at a time or try another direction or tactic. You may have to ask someone for help. But remember that you deserve to succeed, and you are not going to allow yourself to be stopped by this unsuccessful attempt.

The appreciation of your potential will have a dramatic impact on the way you handle success. If you do not appreciate your potential but succeed anyway, you might say to yourself, "I feel fortunate to have gotten this far." If you appreciate your potential, you might say to yourself, "This is a stepping-stone to even greater levels of achievement.

This is just an example of what I can really accomplish in my next effort." If you are unhappy with your present self-image, imagine what your self-image could be and start being happy with the potential while you work towards it. See yourself in the future. Try a lot of different things that you may not succeed at, and soon you'll be looking at all your efforts to achieve as possibilities, not as life or death situations.

START IT NOW!

Notes

Reflective Questions:
1. How can you use negative feedback to achieve your number one goal faster?
2. What are you blaming yourself for?
3. How do you capture your learnings when you take actions?
4. What is your success pattern?

Sample Affirmations
- I use feedback to help me correct my actions so that I achieve my number one goal.
- I have made the decision to be successful.
- I have a positive self-image that is in alignment with my number one goal.
- I am taking action, learning, and making progress toward my number one goal each day.
- I have positive success patterns that are supporting me in achieving my number one goal.

To Close

❧

Setting and achieving goals are a wonderful gift that God has given each of us. The *12 Strategies for Success* is more than a book. It is, in fact, a special tool that will support you in designing the life that you want, need, and desire.

I wish you all the best on your journey to greater success. No matter how old you are or where you are in your life, there are still some things left that you would like to do and wonderful contributions to others that you would like to make.

The good news is that you can, and you will, do those things and make those contributions that are so dear to you and that the world needs.

I wish you all the best, and God Bless you.

CPSIA information can be obtained at www.ICGtesting.com
Printed in the USA
BVOW071607260413

319222BV00001B/1/P